T0119041

To travel is the privilege,
not of the rich but of the imaginative.

NEVILLE

"Neville Goddard was one of the quietly dramatic and supremely influential teachers in the New Thought field for many years . . . In a simple, yet somehow elegant one-hour lecture, Neville was able to clarify the nature of God and God's relationship to every person. He spoke of God in intimate terms as though he knew God very well, which he did."
ROY EUGENE DAVIS

". . . I've read *Resurrection* again and again. Over the years, I've taken ownership of the principles and have achieved all the results that I wanted back then, and much, much more. *Resurrection* contains the revelation that resurrected my life . . . Neville inspired me to find abundance in every part of life and to keep that abundance flowing. I never lost touch with the law, and today I feel that much of my success can be traced to this book."
MARK VICTOR HANSEN

"Neville may eventually be recognized as one of the world's great mystics."
JOSEPH MURPHY, author of
The Power of Your Subconscious Mind

"A popular speaker on metaphysical themes from the late '30s until his death in 1972, Neville authored ten books in which he captured the sheer logic of creative mind principles. His work has impacted me in a very profound way; in fact, he's been a great mentor to me in the past few years."
DR. WAYNE DYER in *Wishes Fulfilled*

"The words of spiritual teacher Neville Goddard retain their power to electrify . . . he captured the sheer logic of creative-mind principles as perhaps no other figure of his era."
Science of Mind magazine

The Power
of
Unlimited Imagination

Neville

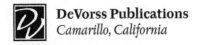

DeVorss Publications
Camarillo, California

THE POWER OF UNLIMITED IMAGINATION
A collection of writings transcribed from lectures by Neville Goddard
by Margaret Ruth Broome

Copyright © 2015 by Victoria Goddard

All rights reserved. No part of this book may be reproduced
or transmitted in any form without permission in writing
from the publisher, except by a reviewer who may quote
brief passages for review purposes.

ISBN: 9780875168791
Library of Congress Control Number: 2014957569
Third Printing, 2024

DeVorss & Company, Publisher
PO Box 1389
Camarillo CA 93011-1389
www.devorss.com

Printed in the United States of America

Table of Contents

Imagination is more important than knowledge.
For knowledge is limited to all we now know and understand,
while imagination embraces the entire world,
and all there ever will be to know and understand.

ALBERT EINSTEIN

Preface

This book, as all things, came into being because of a thought acted upon. Neville left us October 1, 1972, and, since that time, I have invested many hours transcribing the hundreds of tapes I have of his lectures. Neville explained that the ark of life contained and could be understood on three levels: the literal, psychological and spiritual. The lectures that are available deal mainly with the spiritual. However, because those who are now hearing his words on tapes and reading his lectures did not hear him speak on the second (or psychological) level, I realized the need to provide that psychological plane as a foundation for the higher, spiritual level. And so, the thought was planted in my mind. What if there were some lectures that taught this principle on a practical level? Wouldn't it be wonderful if such a series could be found and made available for those who would desire it? And then one day I received a letter from a lovely lady in San Francisco who said she was moving into a retirement home and wanted to send me some notes she had from Neville's lecture series in San Francisco in 1952. These notes constitute this book.

I had a thought. Wouldn't it be wonderful if . . . and acted upon it by feeling the thrill of the thought's completion. I have never met the lady or heard from her since receiving the notes, but I have proved, once again, that imagination (thought) fulfills itself. The living proof is in your hands.

Now, let me tell you a bit about me. Born and raised in a small town in Kansas, I moved to California in 1942 as a good Protestant. But I had a hunger that no organized religion could fill, so I drifted from one belief to another, seeking yet not finding what I was searching for, possibly because I did not know what it was. Then one day I heard a man called Neville, and I knew that, although the outer me did not understand his words, the inner me was singing the Hallelujah Chorus, for I had found the cause of all life: that my very thought, mixed with feeling, was an imaginal act that created the facts in my world.

I remember the first night I lay in my bed and dared to claim, "I AM God." Afraid that the ceiling would crash down on me, I quickly covered my head—just in case. And when nothing happened, I gathered more courage and set out to prove for myself that imagination could create reality. I did not believe it could, and I wanted to prove Neville wrong. That was back in 1964, and I haven't succeeded yet. Not all of my imaginal acts have come to fruition, but I now know that the fault does not lie in the teaching, but in my belief in myself. And, as I have grown in my belief and trust and faith in what I have imagined, I have gained confidence in my own wonderful human imagination.

Several years ago, I put together a group of lectures of Neville's and called the book *Immortal Man*. At the time, I was afraid to change his words even though I felt I could make the message clearer if I did.

Shortly after its publication, I turned to self one night and asked, "Is it all right to change the words as long as I do not change the meaning? I know that if truth were told so that it could be understood, it would be believed. I know your words are true, Neville, but I think I can make them clearer." I fell asleep questioning myself and, in the night, I had this dream:

I am on my way to work. As I enter the building
I see, directly before me, a beautiful restaurant
whose tables are filled with diners, enjoying
their meals. Neville is standing next to a fire-
place, speaking to a group nearby. Thrilled
to find him there, I am eager to show him the
book of his lectures I had just published and
question him regarding the change of words.
But as I turn to take the case I am carrying into
my office, get the book and return, he glances
up and catches my eye. Instantly changing my
mind, I turn and go directly into the restaurant
to join him. But when I arrive, I discover that he
has vanished, leaving the ladies to tell me that
he is gone and will never return again.

Heartsick, I return to the lobby with its
hard, tile floor. Suddenly the case I had been
carrying fell from its handle. The moment it hit
the floor, the case opened, my book fell out and
lay open at its center seam. As I looked down in
horror, I saw that I had been carrying a brief-
case that contained a tape recorder that had
turned on due to the fall, and Neville's voice
was ringing out loud and clear. Embarrassed,
I stooped down to turn off the volume, only

to discover that all the knobs had fallen off the machine and there was no way for me to turn him off. As I tried to push the case over to the far wall in order to pick it up, I awoke with these words ringing in my ears, "I am IN you, AS you."

From that moment on, my fears have vanished and, since that time, I have gained confidence in my writing. These are Neville's words—Neville's thoughts—yet we are so closely woven in the tapestry of thought that the words are now mine.

The lectures you will read are Neville's words, yet they may not be the exact words he spoke back in 1952. The material I had to work with were notes someone had taken in shorthand, transcribed, and duplicated. I have taken the notes and elaborated on them. The words are true and, hopefully, understandable enough so you can test them and discover for yourself that when the truth is applied, it is made alive by a spiritual experience.

Always bear in mind that when Neville speaks of "man," he is speaking of generic man (man/woman). Man is the external world, the natural man; while imagination is the internal world, the man of spirit. God (imagination) became the natural man that the man of nature may become God, who is Spirit.

Always think of yourself as two beings: one who sees through the organs of sense and the other who sees through the mind of imagination. And always remember God's name as he revealed it to Moses. "I AM. That is who I AM. And by this name, I shall be known throughout all generations. I AM that I AM." I the trinity, in unthinkable origin, AM God the Father. And I in creative expression AM the Son, for imagination is born of consciousness. Therefore I, in universal interpretation, in infinite imminence, in eternal procession AM God, the Holy Spirit.

MARGARET RUTH BROOME

THE POWER OF UNLIMITED IMAGINATION

CHAPTER 1

Your Infinite Worth

The purpose of these talks is to bring about a psychological change in you, the individual. Humanity, understood psychologically, is an infinite series of levels of awareness, and you, individually, are what you are according to where you are in the series. Consciousness is the only reality, and where you are conscious of being, psychologically, determines the circumstances of your life. The ancients knew this great truth, but our modern teachers have yet to discover it. There is only one substance in the world. Our scientists call it energy, while scripture defines it as consciousness. We are told that the universe was caused by water, but if this is true, then it could not evolve into anything but water. But if the basic substance is energy (or consciousness), it can be made to manifest itself as iron, steel and wood, to name but a few. Man, seeing a variety of forms, thinks of numberless substances, but what is seen is only a change in the arrangement of the same basic substance—consciousness.

Ephesians tells us that, "All things, when admitted, are made manifest by light." The word "light" recorded here means awareness, consciousness. The state the individual admits into his consciousness is the cause of one man being rich and another poor. The poor man admits to being in the state of poverty by saying, "I am poor," just as the rich man admits wealth by saying, "I am rich." Anything you, an individual, claim yourself to be (be it good, bad or indifferent, right or wrong) must be made manifest in your world, for by claiming the state, you have consented to its life.

There is only one cause, and that is consciousness. Your consciousness is the center from which your world mirrors and echoes the state you presently occupy. Now, a state can be defined as all that you believe and consent to as being true. So, if you want your world to change, you must determine what you want to accept and consent to as true before you can change it. To arrive at a certain definition of self, you must begin by uncritically observing your automatic reaction to an event, for your reaction defines your state. And you can, without getting out of your chair, rebuild your world by changing your level (or state) of being. This is done by observing yourself uncritically as you react to life. If you do not like the circumstances of your life, acknowledge the cause. Be willing to admit that the circumstances are only objectifying what you are conscious of, then change your consciousness and your world will change. If you react to that which is being objectified, you bind yourself to a certain level of awareness, but if you refuse to react, the thread is broken. Stop being conscious of something unlovely, for every unlovely thought causes you to walk in psychological mud. Rather, identify yourself with beauty, with love (the Christ in you), and you will ascend the infinite level of your own being and change the circumstances of your life.

Your state of awareness, like a magnet, attracts life. Steel, in its demagnetized state, is a whirling mass of electrons, but when the electrons are faced in one direction, the steel is magnetized. You do not add to the steel to make it magnetic or take anything away to demagnetize it. This same principle is true for you. You can change your world by rearranging your thoughts and having them travel only in one direction, and that is toward the fulfillment of your desire.

Watch your reactions to life, for any change in the arrangement of your mind that can be detected by self-observation will cause a change in your outer world. It is important to learn to be passive to that which is unlovely and unacceptable to you. In that way, you are awakening the dynamic one within. And when you find your inner being, you will discover that the qualities you condemn in others are really in yourself. Then you will know the secret of forgiveness, for as you forgive yourself, the others are forgiven.

All things (not just a few) are made manifest by the light, and everything manifested is light. The moment you consent to a thought, it is made manifest. It could not come into being unless you consented to its expression by being aware of it. The universe moves with motiveless necessity as it has no motive of its own. Rather, it moves under the necessity of manifesting the arrangements of the minds of men. This teaching is to awaken you to your light, and the awakening begins by self-observation.

If you have a secret affection for living in the mud of self-pity and condemnation, your world will mirror those feelings. But if you will rearrange your mind and live in the heavenly feeling of harmony and love, your manifested world will change. If, today, you would spend five minutes in uncritical observation of yourself, you would be surprised to discover how deceitful you are. It is a terrible shock, I know, but every shock of this type will let in the light of awareness, and life is an ever-increasing illumination. As the light comes in, you become more and more conscious of who you really are.

There is only one cause for the phenomena of life. Only by observing your own consciousness can you discover the cause of what is happening to you. There is no greater tyrant than the belief in a secondary cause. Let that tyrant go by remembering the one and only substance, the only cause, which is awareness, and immediately change what you are aware of. Only by observing your reactions to life can you find yourself. And remember, as long as you react as you do, the same things must confront you, for all that you admit to is made manifest by your consciousness, and everything you manifest is your consciousness.

_Stop walking through the world in the mud
and living in its basement._

Your soul is made up of all that you consent to.

_Lose your soul on one level, and you will find it
on a higher level, defined differently._

_Always examine yourself uncritically,
for the moment you become critical,
you automatically justify your reactions and
associate yourself with the thing observed._

CHAPTER 2

Take Not the Name in Vain

Your individual state of consciousness is your level of being and attracts all of the events you encounter in life. Since your reactions determine what you are, any change in your outer world must be produced by your inner level of being.

In the seventh chapter of the Book of Mark, we are told, "Hear and understand: there is nothing outside which can defile man; but what comes out of a man's mind is what defiles him. He who has ears, let him hear."

Now, thoughts are things. When you identify yourself with a thought, it outpictures itself as an act. If the thought is unlovely, it defiles you. Awaken and select only thoughts that contribute to the birth of your desire. You must constantly observe your dwelling place, for where you are psychologically is what you are. Your mood indicates your state, and you are always externalizing the state upon which you stand.

The Upanishads, one of a class of Vedic treatises dealing with broad philosophic problems, states: "The soul, imagining itself into a state, takes upon itself the results of that state. Not imagining itself into the state, it is free from its results." Your soul is what you consent to. As you feel yourself into the situation of your answered prayer, you have entered a state and your soul has taken upon itself the results of that state. If you do not enter the state, you are free of its lovely results. Accept an idea as true. Identify yourself with it and it will outpicture itself in your world. But if you do not accept the thought and identify yourself with it through feeling, you are free from its results. You must become very selective and learn not to associate yourself with unlovely thoughts.

In the Book of Kings, we are told how those who entered the temple brought something alive with them such as an ox or bullock. These were used as burnt offerings. These sacrifice offerings are your body of suffering. They are the animals you must offer called grievances. No matter what the grievance may be, you have no right to carry it around with you and you cannot ascend in consciousness until all of your grievances are tossed on the altar and sacrificed. Only as you give them up will you find the holy water.

Now, this holy water is not the church variety but the symbol of the twelve aspects of the mind. When your mind is cleared of all of its cobwebs (grievances), the bowl of holy water is placed on the backs of oxen, and your disciplined mind serves you rather than you serving it. The bull symbolizes the mind in its wild state and must be tamed (washed in holy water and clothed in soft raiment). When you enter the holy of holies alone and bathe in its waters, your mind is washed of all mean thoughts and cleansed. Begin now to associate your thoughts only with the good; then that which proceeds out of your mouth (mind) will never defile you.

I AM is the self-definition of the infinite. "Go and tell them that I AM has sent me unto you." Awareness (I AMness) is the only power of the universe. Its power makes you alive. If you say, "I am sick," you are! If you say, "I am secure," you are! Feeling yourself into the situation of a given state, you must take upon yourself the results of that state of mind. All things are made alive from a state of mind, and without the state nothing can be made, as you only resurrect the state from which you are identified. Where you are psychologically is what you are in reality. Therefore, if you catch yourself feeling sorry for yourself, stop it and start feeling happy. If you don't, you will identify yourself with the state of self-pity and outpicture it.

"Let the weak man say, 'I am strong.'" Don't wait until you become strong before saying this. If you feel weak in any sense, affirm "I am strong," and if you persist in that assumption it will harden into fact. No one should ever take the name of the Lord in vain, for that name is I AM.

The righteous man is already conscious of being the person he wants to be. He never sins, but runs into the name, for sinning is missing his desired state, and righteousness is hitting it. "I will set him on high because he knows my name." Assume the consciousness of being the one you want to be and you will be saved from your present state. Your individual hunger can and will be satisfied when you run righteously into the state desired. This is done through the act of feeling. Feel happy and you are conscious of happiness. Feel married and you have consciously moved into the state of marriage. The thing desired must be felt before you are conscious of possessing it.

Learn to say "no" to unlovely thoughts rather than accepting them with passive indifference, for a soul must imagine itself into the act to taste the fruit of the state acted upon. Remember, consciousness alone is the cause of the fruit you reap and the only explanation for its existence.

There is no one to blame but self for all of the things that have happened, are happening, and will happen to you, as they could not come into your world unless you consented to them. Start now to consent only to lovely thoughts of fulfilled desires prior to their confirmation by your senses, and give up the animal instinct of suffering and bathing yourself in the feelings of hurt and self-pity.

The psychological tongue is much like the physical one. If someone annoys you, turn aside and keep the tongue of your mind away from the sore spots of dislike, for your little mental conversations are the producers of your future. Sacrifice your body of suffering by giving it up, and tame your mind, for we are told, "Blessed are the meek (tame), for they shall inherit the Earth." Clothe yourself with joy and good news and you will walk into your holy of holies clothed in your immortal garment of love.

There is a rhythm in your world that you cannot hear or see, and your aura is like no one else's. A bloodhound knows. If two odors were alike, no bloodhound could find you. But you are unique, one of a kind with your own special aura radiating your level of being. Don't judge auras for the simple reason that you have to see the aura of another through your own, and what you are seeing is only your assumption of the man.

Complacency is a curse.

You are given the power of the "I" to think,
and everyone is allowed to think for themselves.

All things, when admitted to consciousness,
are made manifest, be they good, bad or indifferent.

Dare to stand on your own by this teaching and
you will never again feel the need to justify failure.

CHAPTER 3

Desire

As you are, so shall God appear to be to you. The priest will see God as the head of all celestial and terrestrial records. To a judge, he is the great judge forever meting out punishment. To the Hottentot, God is the kind of chief he, himself, would like to be. So, you see, men are forever creating God in their own image.

"God is God from the creation.
Truth alone is man's salvation.
But the God that now you worship
Soon shall be your God no more.
For the soul in its unfolding

Evermore its thoughts remolding
And it learns more truly in its progress
Whom to love and how to adore."

Through this teaching, you will learn to outgrow your concept of God, for God changes not, only your ideas of him change.

Desire is your mainspring of action, for you cannot move without desire. Ask yourself, "What wantest thou of me?" and then formulate your desire. Feel its presence and you have granted yourself the desire's fulfillment. Human life is nothing more than the appeasement of hunger, and the infinite series of levels of awareness is the means to satisfy that hunger. Health is a desire, a hunger that can be appeased when the idea is formulated in the mind that I am healthy. The same is true for wealth, peace, harmony or fame, for all of these are states of awareness. Identify yourself with the state desired. Persist in this identification and, because you and God are one consciousness, what you are conscious of, you outpicture.

The cross is the symbol of suffering. There is no physical cross upon which a man was nailed, but a body of beliefs that a man wears. "Except you deny yourself and lift up your cross and follow me, you are unworthy of me." Lift up your cross by raising your awareness, for your I AMness is the creator of your world.

As an individual, you move and live in time, but your true being is in eternity. Think of the vertical line of the cross as the line of being upon which there are unnumbered levels of awareness. Now, time cannot make you better or wiser. In fact, time cannot do a thing toward changing your level of being, for change is all on the vertical line where you move to higher or lower levels of your own being. Because change is imminent, we speak of it as infinite imminence, as nearer than near and sooner than now. The man you would like to be is imminent. He is nearer than near. The ideal you dream of being is sooner than now and is brought into being by a change in your reactions to life.

In the Book of Revelations, we are told, "I will give to every being according to his work." The only work you are called upon to do is work on yourself. Start this work by observing your reactions to life. Remember, your future is not being developed, it already is. The time track is complete, as well as all of the events you can encounter. As you move up or down the level of your being, changes will occur in your life. You are now resting at a certain level. "Arise, take up your couch and walk," by breaking the threads of life that bind you to the state you are now in. Break these threads by changing your thoughts, for only as you rise within will you find a corresponding change without.

Have you ever wondered what it would be like if you were of too pure eyes to behold iniquity? If you were all tenderness? All love? All generosity? Aim for those feelings and then watch your relationship to them. It is here, in the midst of the storms of life, that you work this law. If you identify yourself with an unlovely state, you will find yourself sinking into it. But you can lift up your cross by breaking your automatic, mechanical reactions to life and sacrificing your present level of being.

This message comes, not to bring peace, but a sword. It comes to set a man at variance against his brother, father, mother and all the members of his household, for I bring the sword of truth that is the word of God. This word is sharper than any two-edged sword, for it is capable of piercing the soul and spirit. I am not suggesting that you turn against your earthly relatives, but that you turn against the psychological ideas that govern your behavior and the dominant mood that governs your actions and reactions to life. If at this moment your feelings are not noble, turn against them, for they are your psychological mother. This is done by putting new feelings in their place. You cannot change your thinking until you change your feeling, and all feelings come from ideas. A man's enemies are those of his own household, which is everything he accepts as true.

This sword can pierce, even to the severing of soul and spirit. Your father (your I AM) is spirit, and when you worship him, you must do so in spirit and in truth. Be still and say to yourself, with feeling, "I AM He."

All that you consent to, all that you believe and accept as true (be it wise or foolish), forms the clothing you wear. But you can be reclothed and ascend to a higher level of being when you take up your cross and follow your imagination.

Most of us are aimless. We want more than we presently have. We want the other fellow to change, but we don't want to do the one thing that will bring the change about, for we don't want to change self. In Revelations, John tells us, "I will give to everyone according to his work." The gift is not given according to the work of another, but according to the work you do on yourself, and that work is to uncritically observe your reactions to life, as they bind you to a certain level. Disassociate yourself from your unpleasant thoughts and associate yourself with your aim, thereby rising to its level, for your ideal is on that vertical line you stand upon.

Scripture tells us to "Seek and you shall find: and when you find him, you will be like him." I tell you, you will never find your fulfilled desire until you are the desire! Those who go searching for love only make manifest their lovelessness, for you never have to search for what you are!

I am Mary and you are Mary too, for we are forever conceiving of ourselves. The whole of human life is the appeasement of desire, and desire, conceived as fulfilled, will externalize itself. If you are not hungry enough to transcend your present level of consciousness, you will not conceive of anything greater. As long as you are in love with the state you are in, you cannot and will not rise from it.

Without the vertical line of states, life would have no meaning. The ancients called this infinite series Jacob's ladder. You do not build this ladder, rather you climb it through self-discovery.

When you think of another, you are seeing only your opinion of him. If you think he is kind, he is kind. If you think he is stupid, he is stupid, as he is playing the part you have assigned him because of your opinion of him. Therefore, if your desire is for him to change, you must change your opinion of yourself, for "he" is only your opinion pushed out.

Where you are psychologically is what you are; therefore, only associate with the feeling that leads you to the fulfillment of your dreams.

May all of your dreams be noble ones.

Pay attention to your thoughts and discipline them so that they flow from the feeling of your wish fulfilled, for you are not awake until the outer you becomes placid, and the inner you dynamic.

Never envy the good fortune of another, simply appropriate your own.

Give yourself your daily bread by giving yourself the opportunity to remember who you are!

CHAPTER 4

Seeing God

S t. Augustine once said, "O, my God, let me see thee, and if to die is to see thee, then let me die that I may behold thy face." Yet, when we fell, God told us, "You cannot see my face and live. But I will cause my glory to pass by and when I pass by, you shall see my back, but my face you will not see." That God is your wonderful I AMness, your awareness who is forever claiming, "I AM, that is who I AM."

Imagination's power is the only power. It is your power to kill, to make alive, to wound and to heal. It is your imagination that forms the light, makes the good and creates the evil, and there is no other God. Man is inclined to believe in two powers, one for good and the other for evil, but I tell you there is only one. The "I" in man is he who kills and makes alive, who curses and creates. Your consciousness of being is the only reality. The self-definition of an absolute state is "I am divine." And this absolute state is God. It is your I AM, which cannot be seen.

Matthew tells us, "Blessed are the pure in heart for they shall see God." The word "pure" in the above statement comes from the Greek word *"katharos,"* which also means, "clean, clear." To be pure, the mind must be cleared of all obstructions created by traditional wrong thinking. The heart must be cleared of the belief in a secondary power. Only when this is done will you be blessed, for you will know the one and only God to be your true self.

There is no power outside of you. The same power in you that makes the good, creates the evil. Start now to free yourself from the belief in two powers, for only then will you be pure in heart and see God.

The whole vast universe is nothing more than the response to the consciousness of men. If you believe that the "I" in another is the cause of your displeasure and not your own "I," then you have planted a tree in your mind that is obstructing your view and must be uprooted. We are told, "No man shall imagine evil in his heart." I am not speaking of a physical organ, but of the mind, the center or heart of the matter. When your heart is pure, you become a member of the order of Melchizedek. Read the story carefully and you will see that when Abraham slaughtered the kings (all of his negative and unlovely ideas), he returned to find Melchizedek, the symbol of the I AM, the being you really are.

Learn to discipline your mind, for only the disciplined mind can maintain the feeling of the wish fulfilled. If what you had imagined has not come into being, it is because you have not severed the ties that bind you to the level where you now stand. You must break your mechanical reaction to life in order to change your life-track.

The only reason for this teaching is to encourage you and push you up the vertical line of the cross. It is very important for you to learn to be uncritical of yourself, for if you are not, you will justify your behavior, which will cause you to remain in your present state. But if you will stop being critical, you will stop the negative thoughts that bind you to your present state and move out of it and into another.

There are three ways to clear your mind of the trees of traditional wrong thinking and allow you to see God. They are: uncritical observation; nonidentification; and sacrifice of the state you formerly believed yourself to be. Man tries to see God by means of little pictures, but God can only be seen through belief in one power. Through uncritical observation, you will encounter your particular state. If you don't like the role the state requires you to play as it unfolds, stop reacting to it. Until you reach the point where you no longer react, you are not pure enough to see God. When you see him, you will know him, as you will be like him.

Where "I" AM is always what "I" AM. Establish one "I" within yourself, not a number of "I"s. The "I" roots out all secondary causes and clears the mind of the power to enslave. Your belief in powers external to you is a tree that must be rooted out of your mind.

Begin now to use this technique and you will realize your every dream. But first you must have a dream, a desire for something, as desire is your springboard of action. Define your objective. If it were fulfilled now, where would you be physically? What would the world look like? Would your wife, husband, mother, father or friends see you differently? Feel their presence, see the joy expressed on their faces and hear their congratulations. Repeat this act until you have the feeling of accomplishment. Then, having assumed the feeling of completion, remain faithful to it, for your assumption contains within itself all of the plans and power necessary for externalization. You need do nothing on the outside, for by your assumption, your mind is being rearranged, and what it confirms, it externalizes. Your desire may be for an improvement in your financial position, your social circle or a deeper understanding of the mystery. The desire is up to you, but when put into practice, this technique will never fail you.

The kingdom of Heaven, with its many states (some lovely and some not so lovely), is within you. The state capable of wounding or healing, killing or making alive, is within you. They are all psychological states, completely furnished and ready to externalize themselves in your world. And, if having entered a particular mansion (state), you do not care to remain there, you may leave it by the same technique it was entered— through the act of assumption.

It is so easy to feel sorry for yourself and so very difficult to give up this feeling. But you cannot enter another state until you do. No one can uproot the weeds of self-pity or the trees of so-called second causes for you. You must uproot them yourself. God put Adam in the garden to tend and keep it. As Adam, you fell

asleep, but when you awake, you are Christ, the power and the wisdom of God. Start now to observe your
reactions to life and do not allow yourself to become
identified with any unlovely state.

Sacrifice your little hurts, your grievances and
belief in secondary causes. Then you will be blessed,
for you will be pure in heart and see God.

Test yourself and you will discover that the fault
you see in the other exists in you. Awaken!

You must free yourself, and the only way to do that is
to awaken the Christ in you who is sound asleep.

Turn to self, and you will find the Christ in you
who is your hope of glory.

CHAPTER 5

Righteousness

I f you have an objective and fail to achieve it, you have sinned, for you have fallen short of your desire. But if you have no desire, you are incapable of sinning. The righteous man, however, being conscious of already having fulfilled his objective, cannot sin.

In the Book of Daniel we are told to "Break off your sin by righteousness." This has nothing to do with any church or ritual, for righteousness is right thinking. In the Book of Genesis the story is told of Jacob's desire to increase his wealth. Lifting his eyes in a dream he beheld the spotted lambs, the ring-striped goats and cattle. Then he said, "I will hold onto my righteousness and not let it go. So shall my righteousness answer for me in time to come."

Follow Jacob's example. Lift up your eyes with a controlled imagination and see what you want to see. Believe in your vision, and your faith will make it solid and real in your manifested world. While sitting in your chair, you can assume the state of consciousness you desire to possess even though your reason and outer senses deny its reality. Then, as Jacob, you can say, "My righteousness shall answer for me in time to come." Jacob knew that he could not become perverse and turn from the new state, but that if he maintained a consciousness of having what reason denied (including the law of genetics), he would achieve his goal.

God the Father is not a man, but the dominant idea that you serve. The enemies of that idea are those of your own household—your own thinking. Hold a dominant idea in your consciousness and, in a way you do not know, your righteousness (right thinking) will cause the desired state to externalize itself in your world.

A Pharisee is one who conforms to all manmade laws; one who strictly observes the Levitical law of "outer purification." Now we are told, "Unless your righteousness exceeds that of the scribes and Pharisees, you will never enter the kingdom of Heaven. But seek ye first the kingdom of Heaven and its righteousness, and all these things shall be added unto you."

True righteousness is consciousness. We confuse the word and seek righteousness as a thing, but the consciousness of being is the magnet that draws a thing to it. Permeate your consciousness with the feeling of being the man (or woman) you want to be, and your righteousness will bring it about.

You cannot inherit Christianity, rather you adopt it. As you come into its inner conviction, you become cleaner and more noble. Christ taught righteousness in his law of identical harvest, saying, "As a man sows, so shall he reap." Taken psychologically, a state of consciousness sown within the mind will be harvested without as external events. And, in like manner, as long as you remain sowing your present state of consciousness, you will continue to encounter similar events in your life.

Walk, conscious of the feeling that your wish is fulfilled, and you will never sin by missing the experience of fulfillment. But you cannot turn away and return to your former state. We are all the prodigal son who went astray. But we are told that when he came to his senses he turned around and entered his Father's house, at which time he was given the fatted calf, the robe and the ring. When you observe who you are in consciousness and come to your senses by turning to your Father (the state desired), it will be given unto you.

Watch your reactions to life and you will discover where you stand psychologically. If your reactions are unlovely, you are walking in the mud and mire, feeding the swine. But when you turn within to the Father of all life and enter the state you desire by assuming its fulfillment, your actions will be lovely. Persist and you will move out of the mud and mire and enter the kingdom of the wish fulfilled.

There is no such thing as righteous indignation, for the wrath of man cannot work righteousness. Nothing so unlovely as righteous indignation could be right consciousness! My goal is to be one who expands in consciousness, for I am a teacher and I must ever grow as a teacher. This is my aim and I must remember it morning, noon and night. I must persist in this state as it externalizes itself in my world.

There is a story told of a little blind girl who had five brothers. The brothers, trusting their senses, went out into the world and lost their way, while the little girl, unable to trust her senses, wove a thread of gold. Attaching one end to her finger, she tied the other to the sun and never lost her way. You, too, can learn to trust the light of consciousness by holding onto the thread that is your aim and not allowing yourself to become enmeshed in the evidence of your senses.

Remembering your desire, you will not get lost like the five brothers as you will not be concerned with what others are doing, but simply walk conscious of being the one you want to be. No power can keep you from your goal when you are conscious of already having attained it.

You are told to "Seek first the kingdom and its righteousness and all these things will be added unto you." The kingdom of Heaven is within you. Turn within and you will find the power to produce what nature and your outer senses deny. Test yourself by controlling your thoughts, by seeing only what you want to see and hearing only that which contributes to the realization that your world is as you want it to be.

If you will keep controlling your world in your imagination until the one sensation crowds out all other ideas, your right consciousness will answer for you and your dream will become your reality. But, if you don't feel fulfilled, you can easily be diverted and miss your mark.

The Bible's teaching is one of rising higher and higher in consciousness until rebirth occurs. There is but one purpose in life, and that is to rise higher and higher on the vertical bar of the cross.

Knowing the state you desire to express, walk as though you are now expressing it. "No man, having put his hand to the plow, looks back." In other words, once you have moved into the new state, do not look back at the old state or you will become as Lot's wife. She looked back and was turned into a pillar of salt, which is a preservative. The moment you look back at your former state, you re-enter it, as all states exist, preserved in your imagination and ready for occupancy.

The kingdom of Heaven is a higher state of awareness, a step above where you now stand, and each higher level is reached by a change of attitude for the better. There is not a problem that cannot be resolved by a change of consciousness. And that which requires a state of awareness to produce its effect can never be affected without that state. It is the height of folly to expect security while being conscious of insecurity. On the other hand, you cannot be insecure if you walk conscious of being secure.

You don't have to "pull strings" to get what you want; all you need do is walk in the consciousness of already having it. For an assumption, though false, if persisted in, will harden into fact. Don't try to be a better man, but, try to be better at something. Most metaphysical students have no aim, claiming God knows best. But, I ask you, how can this be when you and God, your Father, are one?

Human nature wants the thing to come first with belief to follow. But I say, you must assume the consciousness of already having (or being) your desire before the sign that you have it can appear. Signs follow; they do not precede. Seek the conscious feeling of having already reached your goal, and the sign that you have achieved it will follow.

"Be transformed by the renewing of your mind"
by changing the ideas planted there, for you cannot
change your thinking until you change the ideas
from which your thoughts flow.

You don't get things and then become righteous;
righteousness is right seeing.

Always claim the level above the one you are now on
by dying to your present level,
for your Father's house has many mansions.

Let go of your present mansion and
reach for the one you seek!

CHAPTER 6

The Perfect Will of God

Understood psychologically, humanity is an infinite series of levels of awareness, and the individual is what he is according to where he is in the series. In the Book of Romans Paul urges us to "Be not conformed to this world, but be transformed by the renewing of your mind that you may prove what is good and acceptable, the perfect will of God." In other words, do not look at the external world and call it reality, but break its spell by transforming your thinking. But you can't change your thinking until you change your ideas, for it is from ideas that you think. Remember, your level of awareness attracts life and is the sole cause of the phenomena you observe.

To be aware is to do the will of God whose name is I AM. Always being aware, what you are aware of is what you are. "I AM (aware of) that (which) I AM." Think of an infinite scale of values as I AM, with your desired state just above where you now stand. God speaks to you through the language of desire. When you wish to ascend, it is because God is speaking, calling upon you to surrender yourself to the feeling of already being what you want to be. Let go of fear, limitation and doubt and subject yourself to the will of God. A mere assumption will lift you up to the level upon which your ideal is identified, and you will begin to see your world differently. This is where self-observation comes in. You do not observe the outer world, but your reactions to it.

When another displeases or offends you, look within to the "I" who heard with displeasure and is expressing it. It is difficult to believe, I know, but you alone are the cause of your displeasure. A lady I know thought her employer was a monster and impossible to please. She had formed an opinion of him and that invisible and inaudible opinion spoke to her all day long, causing her boss to do what he did and say the words to cause her displeasure. Being a gracious lady and willing to change her feeling of "I," she heard her boss praise her and she thanked him for his praise. The moment she found herself returning to the old role of criticizing him, she stopped the thought and put on the new record of praise, thanks and congratulations. Within twenty-four hours, the new record externalized itself and, when she resigned a year later, her boss begged her to stay and told her that if she ever wanted to return, the door was always open to her.

Your inward conversations are the breeding ground of all your future action. Morning, noon and night you are carrying on internal arguments. When you catch yourself, break the habit by consciously creating new thoughts, thereby making a new record to externalize itself in your future.

God's will is I AM. His will is always being done, for it is the power that resurrects and makes alive. There is no transforming power in time, only transformation of the moment. If you are having difficulty with another, look into self, for it is the "I" called you who is speaking to you as a thought. Listen carefully to what you are saying to yourself and you will discover where the difficulty lies.

Let me now define "self" or "soul." It is that which you believe, feel, think and consent to. You may consent to the belief that you have been mistreated, that you are dumb, or they, in their cruelty, are causing your displeasure. If you do, your consent forms your level of being and attracts your life, be it good, bad or indifferent. Your soul cannot be changed by joining churches, synagogues or groups. You must turn to self, the inner "I" you know so well, as it is he who attracts those who mistreat you and determines every little detail of your outer experience.

If you have a secret affection for your conflicts, you cannot be helped. But, when you consent to be otherwise, then you can change. Subject yourself to the will of God by first knowing your ideal, then yielding to it by doing in your imagination what you would do physically if your desire were realized. Once this is clearly defined, repeat the act over and over again until you feel affected by it and its fulfillment possesses your mind. When the idea is so firmly entrenched and your thoughts flow freely from it, watch, for you will have a change in your external world.

Become pure in heart by purging your mind from the belief in powers outside of yourself. Then, believing that consciousness is the only reality, weave yourself into a new state of awareness. For your world is your house, your state of consciousness externalized. Clean house by observing your thoughts. When you first begin to do this, you will discover most of your thoughts are unlovely. But, as you learn to passively think of people you dislike, your thoughts will lose their unloveliness and, with a mind filled with joy and thanksgiving, you will ascend Jacob's ladder of self into the kingdom of love.

When you have carefully defined your desire, completely and utterly yield to it. Then try to remain faithful to the new idea you have entered. In the beginning you may not succeed, but don't condemn yourself. Simply return as many times as necessary until the feeling becomes so strong, your thoughts habitually flow from the new state.

This teaching is not for the weak. It is not for those who seek escape from life or want to point fingers of blame at one another. To find the Christ in you who is your hope of glory, you must be willing to test yourself. I tell you, he is your "I" who calls all men and manifestations to you. Life is easier when you can blame another, but I urge you to pray, not for an easy life but to become a stronger man. The one who is bearing witness to your thoughts is the cause of your misfortune, not the other fellow. Be transformed by the renewing of your mind and you will prove the good and acceptable word of God.

Would it be acceptable to you to be lifted on high? That is the will of God, which will not turn back until he has executed and accomplished the intents of your mind. You are doing God's will when you identify yourself with your desire. And, if you believe your claim, you are righteous and your world will outpicture your righteousness. But if you do not believe, you will miss your mark and die in your sins.

The only escape from the life you now lead is by a radical psychological transformation of self. This is done by defining your "I" with your desire, then changing your thoughts until their effect possesses your mind and your "I" resides comfortably in the new state. Remember, your level of being attracts life, and unless the level changes your history remains the same. Let your present level die by subjecting your entire being to a level beyond it. Try it. It really is not difficult to do.

Remove the hold that past wrong emotional reactions have upon you by reviewing the experiences and changing them. This is done by rewriting the experience in your mind and saying what you should have said and doing what you should have done at the time. Let this corrected picture slip back into the subconscious as you resolve not to make the same mistake again. By repetition of this technique, you will rid yourself of all feelings of hate, resentment and other emotional disturbances that cling to your memory. And, to the degree that you release yourself from these destructive feelings, you will free yourself from their power to attract ill health and wrong results.

*Relaxation of the body, passivity of the mind
and fixation of attention on the objective desire
equals fulfillment of the objective.*

Anxiety has no creative power.

*Consciousness (whose origin is in eternity)
provides the power for your experiences in time.*

*Test yourself, for in this teaching
there is no room for failure.*

CHAPTER 7

Be Ye Doers of the Word

I n the Book of Hebrews Paul tells us to "Rest in the Lord." Why? Because the man who rests in the Lord is transformed into the image in which he rests. If my aim is to be a good teacher and I rest in that feeling, I will be transformed into that image.

Unfortunately, most of the states in which men rest are negative. Feeling insecure, you will rest in the conviction that the world owes you a living. Feeling hurt, it is easy to rest in that grievance until your mood becomes natural. You may condemn the state and believe others to be its cause, but, through your feelings of being hurt, you will be transformed into the very image of the state you condemn. And if someone seems to cause you displeasure, remember, there is no other. The state in which you rest is causing you to listen to silent and invisible conversations. Although the words are heard by you and you alone, they act as magnets and draw to you the circumstances of your life.

"Be ye doers of the word and not hearers only, deceiving yourselves." Every meeting I share with you the knowledge I have gained through personal experience, but I cannot make you put this knowledge into practice. As a teacher, I demand results. As a student, I urge you to test this truth, for if it is true it will prove itself in the testing.

In the twenty-fifth chapter of the Book of Matthew the parable is told of the servants who were given talents by their master. One was given five talents that he increased to ten. Another, two talents were given that were increased to four. And when the third received his one talent, he buried it, thereby never allowing it to increase. When the master returned, he rejoiced at the increase he was shown by the first two. But he took from the one who had placed his talent in hiding and gave it to the one who had ten, saying, "To everyone who has, more will be given and he will have abundance; but from him who has not, even that which he has will be taken away."

This teaching is like the talents. Practiced daily, your power of awareness will grow. If you are a hearer only, your knowledge, not used, will soon wither away and atrophy. Test yourself every day. Leave the other fellow alone and turn to self, for the promise is, "According to your work will it be done unto."

The man who overcomes himself rises to a higher level of being. Uncritically, observe your reactions to life, then work on yourself by practicing this psychologically. Only by working on self can you rise to a higher level. But you cannot do it with a negative emotion; it must be a positive one. We are told to "Lift up your eyes unto the hills from whence cometh your help." Negative thoughts cause downward emotions, while positive thoughts elevate. If you listen to your thoughts, stop their negative flow and change them so that you are hearing what you want to hear, you will feel a positive emotion of relief that is followed by a stillness that brings with it the knowledge that your prayer has been answered.

Now, as the title of this lesson implies, we are urged to be doers of the word and not hearers only, deceiving ourselves. In the Book of James, a hearer is defined as like a man who observes his natural face in the mirror, then turns and forgets what he looks like; whereas the doer is one who looks into the perfect law of liberty, perseveres and is blessed in all that he does.

How do you go about looking into the mirror of the mind and being pleased with what you see? By looking into the face of your wife, husband, parent or friend. Close your eyes, relax and think of a friend who would rejoice in your good fortune. Tell him your good news and watch the expression of joy appear on his imagined face. His expression will liberate you, as his knowing has set you free to express your desire. Having looked into the perfect law of liberty, persevere and you will be blessed in the doing.

In the Book of Matthew the law is stated thus: "Whatever you wish that men would do to you, do so to them, for this is the law of the prophets." Here we discover that the Bible is speaking of a man's psychology and not his physical form. The Bible records what you do within yourself, telling you that the conversations carried on internally are the breeding grounds of your future actions. Forever carrying on mental conversations with imaginary beings, become aware of your thoughts. Be selective and make your inner conversations positive, for the mechanical imagination is asleep and negative, while the awakened imagination is positive and noble.

Tonight, single out someone you love and rearrange your opinion of him. Carry on mental conversations with him based upon this new premise and you are a doer of the word. If you don't, you are a hearer only, deceiving yourself.

This teaching is to awaken you to the active, dynamic being that you really are. Asleep, your thoughts are negative and passive and cannot change until you uncritically observe your reactions to life. If you are honest with yourself, you will find an internal being you are not proud of, a monster that needs taming. Tame that monster by filling your mind with positive thoughts of joy and fulfillment, and you will turn that monster into a being of love.

Get into the habit of observing your reactions to life. Give yourself your daily bread by giving yourself the ability to no longer react negatively. Become a doer by recognizing a negative thought, then breaking it and going immediately to a positive one. All of your grievances, your hurts, self-pity and beliefs that others are the cause of your sorrow are animals that need to be sacrificed on the altar of consciousness. Letting all negative feelings go, select the mansion (state) you desire to enter and go in.

The law that brings poverty into being also brings

wealth. Let the weak man say, "I am strong," and the poor man say, "I am rich," for only that which you affirm within yourself can be outpictured. Feel yourself into the state of poverty, and poverty is outpictured. Feel yourself into the state of security by saying, "I am secure," and security will result. But if you do not feel yourself into the state desired, you will be forever free of its results, as that which requires a state of consciousness to produce its effect will never be affected without such change in consciousness. You must feel yourself right into the situation of your answered prayer, then live and act in that conviction. If you don't, you will never know the results of that state.

Your fortune or misfortune was brought into being by your state of consciousness. There is no other cause. Have the courage to accept this and then become a doer and, in so doing, be blessed in your every deed. Start now to become conscious of what you hear yourself say to yourself and stop receiving those impressions mechanically and unconsciously. What you hear must be filtered through what you are. And what you are is what you hear. Kind thoughts stem from kind ideas created by a kind person; therefore, be kind to one another, tenderhearted and forgiving.

Now, an assumption is called the crown of the

mysteries and every assumption is made by you alone. The world you see depends, not so much on what is there, as on the assumption you make when you look at it. The talent entrusted to you is your power of conscious assumption. Don't bury it! Asleep to this knowledge, your reactions to the day are mechanical, negating everything you see and hear.

*Become conscious of what you are doing
and saying to yourself. Awake!*

*Rise in consciousness by controlling your thoughts
and making them positive, kind, loving and fulfilling.*

*Control your imagination with steady attention
and dare to stand and be heard.*

*Think noble thoughts based on noble concepts
and they will pay great dividends, for you will rise
in consciousness and transform your world.*

CHAPTER 8

The Pearl of Great Price

When you possess the mind of Christ, you are in possession of the pearl of great price! That pearl is imminent. It is nearer than near and sooner than now, for the pearl of great price is your own wonderful human imagination. You have always possessed this mind but, like every possession, unless you know it is yours and are willing to use it, it is nonexistent to you. Believe me, everything in your world was first conceived in your imagination. The house you live in, the car you drive, the clothes you wear, as well as your friends, your loved ones, your enemies and the strangers on the street were imagined before externalized. Now it is time to control your human imagination and govern it by love. I urge you to awaken to the discovery that everything you seek in time is contained within you.

There is only one mind with unnumbered levels of awareness. Your level determines where you are and what you are; for what you think, you are. This mind is not something detached from you but your own lovely imagination, the body of the Father and the only redemptive power in the universe. It can save you from your present state or bind you to it.

Christ is defined in scripture as the power and wisdom of God—nourishment for you as your hope of glory. All things are made by this power. Without God-nourishment not anything is made, for Christ, who is your own wonderful human imagination, is yourself! Looking with the human eye, you see a world outside and seemingly independent of your perception. But when you view the world through the "I" of imagination, you understand its meaning. Turn within and test yourself and you will discover that you are your own savior. Then you will begin to assert the supremacy of your human imagination. You will cease to bow before the dictates of the world without and start to put your dreams into effect.

A tamed man is one who is self-disciplined. Tame

yourself by observing yourself. Are you wasting your strength in negative emotions? If so, then discipline yourself out of the muck and mire you have been living in and rise, with your disciples, into a state of joy and the body of love. Do this, and you will have found the pearl of great price.

In this world, you appear to be a man (or woman) of flesh and blood. Your father, mother, sisters and brothers are known. But I tell you, you are far greater than the greatest man on Earth, for you are Jesus Christ.

Imaginative love is sleeping in your body of flesh. Awaken the love that you are by claiming that your mind is Christ. Claim your pearl of great price, for it is the key that will unlock the treasure house of Heaven. With your mind as Christ, you will discover that you are no longer capable of thinking unlovely, negative thoughts and will have no desire to retaliate.

The Bible is your biography, for you are Jesus, the great Jehovah of the Old Testament who finds fulfillment in the New. Using the mind of man, you are asleep. It is time to awaken, to cast off the mind of man who says, "I can," "I was" or "I will be," and assert your divine inheritance that is the mind of God who says, "I AM." Nothing is impossible to God, and nothing is impossible to you when you claim to be the mind of God.

When you know what you want, ask yourself where you would sleep if you had it. What would your world look like? Would a friend be happy for you? With the answers to your questions filling your mind, fall asleep in your desired place. View the world from that vantage point and hear your friend rejoice now that your desire is a physical fact. Then believe in Christ—the power to put all things under your subjection—and it will be done unto you.

Remember, there is no such thing as a powerful fate to which you must bow, nor do you have to accept life on the basis of the world without. Turn to self. Claim your pearl of great price and remember:

> "What seems to be, is to those to whom
> It seems to be, and is productive of the
> most dreadful consequences to those to
> whom it seems to be;
> Even of Torments, Despair and Eternal
> Death."

WILLIAM BLAKE

*This world is like a machine whose actions
and reactions are automatic.*

*Separate yourself from this machine-like mind
and use your wonderful human imagination to
rise to higher and higher levels of your own being.*

*If you do not like the events of your life,
change them by controlling your imagination.*

*Awaken to the discovery that everything you seek
in time is contained within you.*

CHAPTER 9

Self-Remembering

D o you have a goal in life? An aim for yourself? If you do, start now to lift yourself to its level by the act of self-remembering. Do not try to be a better man or woman, but transcend your present level of being by being better AT something. Your goal should be so important that you cannot forget it and your hunger for its externalization so intense that you cannot and will not let the thought go until it is embodied in flesh.

Scripture tells us, "Many are called, but few are chosen." The word "chosen" means to separate, to choose, to decide. Every day, you are offered the opportunity to choose a new idea, to enter a new state from which to think and feel. Unnumbered emotions and thoughts are yours to call forth but, because of the aim with which you desire to be identified, only a few emotions and thoughts are chosen. Begin to rise within yourself by letting go of your former beliefs and restrictions. Choose the thoughts and emotions you desire to express and enter your desire through the act of feeling.

In the eleventh chapter of Mark, two disciples were told to "Go into the village where you will find a colt tied at the crossroad upon which no one has sat. Loose him and bring him to me. If anyone says, 'Why are you doing this?' say, 'The Lord has need of him.' Then he mounted the unbridled ass and rode into the city of Jerusalem."

Now, the animal found at every crossroad is not a colt or an ass but the individual's permanent, predominant emotion. Desiring to express a new emotion, you may find it difficult to ride. But you will always find your emotions tied at the crossroads of life. If you have never felt secure before, you may not be able to ride the animal emotion of security for more than a few seconds at a time. But the important thing is to try, for controlled imagination can ride any emotion into the city of peace: the embodiment of the ideal state.

An emotion is right or wrong relative to a desire. If you feel uneasy as you commit yourself to your desire, you are walking in the wrong direction and will never reach it. But if the feeling is natural (right), and you persist in your assumption, it will become a fact. At times, even when your aim feels natural, you may allow doubts to creep in, and move away from your goal. When this happens, don't condemn yourself, simply get back on that emotion and ride it again, for the beast is unbridled and must be ridden until you and it become one. Acknowledge the feeling of importance, of security or of being dignified within yourself, for your consciousness is reality. What you are conscious of being right now, you are. If you desire to be other than what you are, remember, the state desired is just as real as the one you are conscious of now. Enter the new state by becoming conscious of being it. Persist! Find the feeling of the new state and ride it into Jerusalem.

Scripture calls upon man to remember himself by associating himself with his aim and walking in its direction. Only as you discipline yourself can you embody your aim. In his eleventh chapter Mark makes this statement, "Whatever you desire, believe that you have received it and you will. And whenever you stand praying, forgive." How do you fulfill a desire and forgive another? By finding the quality you thought to be in another and removing it from yourself. Then place the feeling you desire to express in its place. When this has been done, you have risen right into the state of your answered prayer.

Now, prayer is conditioned upon the belief that it is already answered. Desire is your springboard. Standing upon your desired state, you may discover that the board wobbles or the ground sways beneath your feet. But if you persist in being conscious of having attained your desire, even though your reason and outer senses deny it, what you are conscious of will become your reality.

Tonight, form a lovely aim for yourself and feel its fulfillment. Associate yourself with that feeling by becoming conscious of it. Do that and you will bless and be blessed by God who is your very self. Say to yourself, "I and my Father are one." Your inner being is he who men call God. He is never so far off as even to be near, for He is your own wonderful human consciousness.

All things, when admitted into your consciousness, are made manifest by its light, but something must be admitted first. If you are conscious of being beaten, the thought will manifest itself and you will be. Do you feel insecure? If you do, and persist in that mood, you will sink into its slums, for everything manifested is consciousness externalized.

What thought dominates your mind right now? Regardless of what it is, you have consented to it, but you need not perpetuate it. The thought that enters the mind does not defile you. You may consent to any thought, be it one that defiles or blesses you when it goes forth. But every thought will be made manifest. The state in which you presently reside was only a thought before you entered it, just as is the state you now desire, and it can just as easily be realized. Take the challenge. Formulate your aim and rise in consciousness to its fulfillment. Think it is real and it is, for everything is possible to a thought.

Self-remembering is remembering your aim, so in the course of a day you should ask yourself where you are psychologically. Your reality lives in a psychological country where you can walk in the mire, the valley, or the mountaintops. Choose this day the state you desire to enter. Feel its mood and acknowledge its fulfillment. Walk faithful to that assumption and, although your reason and your senses deny it, your persistence will cause it to become a fact.

Life will become easier when you are brutally frank with yourself and acknowledge your reactions

to that which was created by you and is being reflected
to you. Resolve to react only in a positive manner. Positive thoughts produce positive effects.

As you see your world differently, your consciousness changes, thereby changing future events.

You, all imagination, are the sum total of your reactions to life.

This is the only cause and explanation of the events you encounter.

If you do not like your world, change your reaction to it.

CHAPTER 10

Your Destiny

Love is the only true power, and your power is in proportion to your love. When scripture speaks of the violent taking the kingdom by storm, it is not referring to violent characters, but the power of love, which gives the force necessary to rise to a higher level of awareness.

There is no ultimate destiny for (understood psychologically) life is everlasting. It is the appeasement of a hunger whose main force is desire. Man rises on the springs of his desire, with every level of the vertical line of the cross within him so organized that it will lift him, through desire, to higher and higher levels of himself.

I, like all true teachers, teach the art of overcoming the violence that characterizes mankind's present level of being. In many ways, we have advanced beyond our forefathers, but we have remained just as violent as they. It is my wish for you that you break your violent, negative nature. For if you will, you will rise in consciousness and find your destiny waiting for you. Every moment in time you are offered the chance to prove your ability to overcome violence. How? By assuming that consciousness is the only reality and that nothing has reality save the consciousness you have of it. In that assumption, you will find the sole cause of the phenomena of life.

Your reactions to life define you, and as long as they remain as they are, your life will stay the same. Your world is but a projection of your state of awareness. Consciousness is the only substance and the only cause of the phenomena of life; therefore, it is impossible for change to occur until there is a change in consciousness.

All that you consent to, be it good, bad or indifferent, is projected into your world through your "I" of awareness. If security is your aim, you must establish an awareness of security so strong that you can feel it and say within yourself, "I am secure." You are free to consent to violence and grievances or security and peace of mind. Whatever you consent to by becoming aware of it will be yours. Your aim is always just above the state where you now stand. Throughout the day, ask yourself if you are conscious of your aim, and you will discover how near or how far you are from it. If you are not conscious of being secure at the moment, claim that you are. Persist, and maybe tomorrow as you observe your day, you will find the awareness growing stronger and stronger.

Learn to stand alone by claiming, "I am what I am because I am conscious of being it." Stop looking at others and start observing your reactions to their behavior. Turn within and change your violent nature to one of love. Do that and you will ascend the ladder of life and reach your destiny. It is impossible to embody a new level of thought through the efforts of another. The rock upon which you must stand is consciousness. All other ground is sinking sand.

It is the height of folly to expect the incarnation of a new concept to come out of the evolutionary process. The thing you are seeking must be incarnated before it can be made visible. There is a wide difference between knowing something mentally and knowing it spiritually. I can teach you the law of identical harvest.

You can read how to apply the law through my books and mentally know the steps necessary to have wealth, but you will never know wealth, spiritually, until you consciously say within yourself, "I am wealthy." A man is sick because he is conscious of being so. Let the sick man say, "I am well," the hungry man say, "I am full," and the troubled man say, "I am at peace," and their right consciousness will produce that which they are conscious of being. If you want to know what love is, you must become loving, for you cannot know a thing until you are it.

I am teaching the art of Being: the art of spiritually knowing a state. In the Book of Joel, we are told, "Let the weak man say, 'I am strong.'" This applies not only to the physical body but to every facet of your being. Seek to know your desire spiritually, for only when the spirit feels the naturalness of the desire will it project itself in your outer world. Always remember, you will never experience what you refuse to affirm as true of yourself!

Awaken! Become ever more aware of what is taking place within you. Lift up your cross and, without turning to the left or the right to ask another, turn within and consciously claim your aim, then watch it harden into fact.

If you do not apply my words, you remain right where you are, for you must be a doer in order to be blessed with your deeds. Desire is hidden identity, as you already are what you want to be. "Never would you have sought me had you not already found me." The level of being you seek can be found by changing your reactions to life to conform to the level you wish to express. It is not necessary to use pressure, pull strings or ask anyone to aid you.

All you need do is change your attitude. After clearly defining your aim, sincerely observe your inner conversations and your reactions with regard to them. When your thoughts and reactions are disciplined, your "I" will lift you to your higher level and fulfill your aim.

Your fellow man is not to be condemned, but awakened. This is done by awakening yourself. As you rise in consciousness, you take all men with you. Think of your wonderful human imagination as the vertical line of the cross, limitless, with time as the cross section. You are free to ascend (or lift up) the cross, but you cannot rise until you deny your limitations. Christianity is a way of life. With your mental eyes wide open, adopt Christianity by becoming aware of what it is.

No matter how reasoning justifies acts of violence,

don't accept them. If you do, you contribute to the state, and it is a state you do not want to experience. Clear your mind of the trees of traditional thinking. Become pure in heart and you will see that consciousness is all and all is consciousness. You will discover that the state you are conscious of being is the state made manifest.

*If you do not like what you are encountering
in life, rearrange your thoughts
by changing your consciousness.*

*Form the state you desire and occupy it in your mind.
This is how you transform self.*

*As you yield to the state desired, watch your world.
It will transform itself into the ideal
held in consciousness.*

*Where you stand, the ground is holy,
for you are the temple of the living God.*

CHAPTER 11

Your Personal Autobiography

The Bible, the most wonderful book in the world and the most misunderstood, is your personal autobiography. It is not the recording of historical events as your teachers teach, and its writings were never intended to be interpreted as such. The persons recorded there never existed, and the events never happened on Earth. The Bible is speaking of the Heaven within and the Earth without.

Its story begins: "In the beginning, God created the Heaven and the Earth. And the Earth was without form and void; and darkness was upon the face of the deep. Then the Spirit of God said, 'Let there be light,' and there was light." The light spoken of here comes from Heaven, which is within you. The light that shines upon your Earth is the light of your consciousness and shines from within you. The outer man (called the Earth) is dark, while the inner man (called Heaven) is the being who was in the beginning with God and was God but is sound asleep. As your autobiography, the Bible tells how you are lifted up from your present level of being into a higher one.

In the Old Testament, we find the Pentateuch (the first five Books, as the law of Moses). These books were written in 500 BC, while the earliest date known for the New Testament is AD 170. The first known New Testament did not include the Epistles to the Hebrews or the Books of Peter and James. (It is James who speaks of the double-minded man, declaring that he can receive nothing from the Lord.) Then we had the Apocrypha, which consisted of early Christian writings that were excluded from the Jewish and Protestant Old Testament. These writings give four biographical sketches of a principle, rather than a man. It took nine hundred years for the Bible to come into its present form. So when you read it, always bear in mind that it is speaking of the kingdom of Heaven within you. It is telling of a revelation of an eternal principle called Christ, who is your hope of glory. All of the characters recorded in scripture are aspects of your mind that you will discover as you fulfill your destiny, which is to fulfill scripture within yourself.

No man named Moses ever wrote any commandments on stones; rather the word "stone" means "literal truth." The literal-minded man comes first and is given certain laws to live by, thus blocking psychological truth. As long as you see things on the outside as facts, your mind is blocked and you are unable to grasp their psychological meanings. But when you become thirsty for the truth and begin to apply the law, the spirit of God will move upon this psychological sea of understanding and your life will take that truth (water) and turn it into wine. In the state of Moses, God's true name is revealed to you. Take his name (your I AM) as your rod of understanding and hit the stone of literal truth with it, and psychological water will come forth. Drink it by putting my words into practice and you will convert the psychological water of truth I have given you into the wine of the spirit.

Now, the clothing spoken of in scripture is that of the mind and not of the body. John the Baptist is described in the third chapter of Matthew as one called Elijah in 2nd Kings. It is said he wore a garment of

camel's hair and a leather girdle around his waist. Hair
and skin are the most external things a man possesses; therefore, John the Baptist represents the outer
man who has not yet clothed himself internally. Jesus
is the inner man. He wears the seamless garment woven from above, and those who wear his garment are
always found in the king's house.

The New Testament teaches a complete and radical transformation of self and calls it rebirth, but John
the Baptist calls it repentance and urges us to change
our thinking of the kingdom of Heaven. It is said that
he lived in the wilderness with the wild animals. Well,
you are John, living in the wilderness where you have
no direction of your own and allow your animal emotions to run wild. But when you begin to tame your animal instincts and call them into discipleship, strength
will come to you from within and you will be baptized
in the water of truth.

Speaking in a parable, Matthew likens the kingdom of Heaven to a sower who sows his seeds on different types of soil. The sower spoken of here is not a
being external to yourself, for you are the sower and
the seed. Your own wonderful human imagination is
God, the sower who said, "Let us make man in our image," then fell asleep and annexed the brain of the out-

er man as the seed for his redemption. As Adam (or the red earth), man is the psychological earth upon which the kingdom of Heaven is planted. In the parable, we are told that when one hears the word but does not understand it, the evil one comes and snatches away that which is sown in his heart. But he who hears with understanding, bears fruit and yields a hundredfold.

Another parable is told comparing the kingdom of Heaven to a man who, having sowed good seeds in his field, fell asleep and his enemy came and sowed weeds there. These weeds are false teachings, planted in the mind, false beliefs and concepts that can be bound and burned when you turn within to discover the truth and the kingdom of Heaven to be yourself.

In the eleventh chapter of Genesis, the story is told of how the tower of Babel is built with stone (literal truth) and bricks (manmade concepts). Before the building was erected, there was only one language and few words, but during the building, confusion reigned, and soon no one understood the language of the other. This tower exits today as the little mystical, occult groups of the world. You have no enemies save those of your own household. Making truth of false teachings, you believe that your security depends upon the money you have in the bank; or your health depends upon the pills you take; or your happiness depends upon another. In so doing, you build your own tower of Babel. But I say to you, your consciousness of being is the only reality of the state you are in, and all of the enemies of that state are within you. In his beatitudes, Matthew tells you that your attitude of being is blessed when it is clothed in soft raiment, for when you wear the seamless garment of imagination, you are free to rise higher and higher into the Garden of Eden within you. You are the gardener of your mind, where you plant the seeds of your own selection. As the Man of Imagination, become conscious of being that which you have planted, and your harvest will be a hundred-fold, for you always become what you behold.

In his sixteenth chapter, Matthew tells the story of the Pharisees and Sadducees who, unbelieving, ask for a sign from Heaven. Then we are told to take heed and beware of the influences of the Pharisees and Sadducees. Now, these are not men, but attitudes of mind. If you believe that you must live in the "right" neighborhood; that you must know the "right" people; that your skin must be the "right" color; or that you must be in the "right" place at the "right" time, your attitude is what scripture calls a Pharisee. Beware of that kind of thinking, for the road to a higher level of self is always internal and never external.

Mark tells us that the kingdom of Heaven is like a merchant of fine pearls who finds a pearl of great price, sells all that he has and buys it. As long as you hold onto one thought of something external to your own mind, you do not have enough money to buy the pearl of great price. You must be willing to sell all belief in anything outside of self. The road to the kingdom leads upward and is always in an internal direction. You cannot travel this road wearing clothes made of skin and hair. You must be clothed in your wedding garment, which is always woven from within.

Again, we are told that the kingdom of Heaven is like a net that is cast into the sea and gathers fish of every kind, be they good or bad. When it is brought ashore, the good are placed into vessels and the bad thrown away. Become discriminating. Select your thoughts carefully and throw away any unlovely and negative ones. Allow only that which is of good report to fill your mind and you will be the good fisherman. In this same thirteenth chapter of Matthew, the question is asked, "Have you understood this?" It is my prayer that every one of you will answer, and say, "Yes."

Now it is said, "Do not put new wine into old wineskins, for the skins will burst and the wine spilled, and the skins destroyed; but put new wine into fresh wine-skins so both are preserved." Old thoughts, the traditions of men, the belief in power outside of self are the old wineskins that must be burst to allow the beliefs to be spilled and destroyed. New wine, gained by the fulfillment of God's promise within, must be poured into your consciousness (fresh wineskins) so that both are preserved.

Man does not evolve on the outside. There is only one presence, only one essence in man, called Christ, and defined as God's power and your hope of glory. This power can be awakened if you, God's word, are not tarnished by the belief in a power outside of self. Awaken! Give up all false beliefs and clothe yourself in the soft raiment of an internal attitude that implies the fulfillment of your dream. The Bible, from beginning to end, is the psychological story of your soul and tells you that the first thing you must do is change your thinking. I bring to you a new idea relative to the cause of the phenomena of life, telling you that you are not what you believe yourself to be, but possess possibilities of infinite inner growth.

Be your attitude good, bad or indifferent, when you clothe yourself in an attitude, its fulfillment is not dependent upon anything external to you. But when you depend upon external laws to determine your attitude, you are on the level of Elijah and John the Baptist. Their teaching was wonderful, but it was stone, and the state was a violent one. John the Baptist cannot enter the kingdom of Heaven. You must overcome his state by consciously turning within and disciplining your internal attitudes. This is your destiny. You are destined to awaken within yourself as you climb Jacob's ladder of states to higher and higher levels of your own being. The state of awareness you desire to express must be bought by selling all of your beliefs in any external power to help you. Once free from their encumbrance, you will move in faith into your desired state.

In the Book of John, Jesus, as a teacher, makes this statement: "Let not your heart be troubled; you believe in God; believe also in me." Then he adds this thought: "It is expedient that I go, lest the comforter will not come." Here we see a teaching that is seemingly taught from without, but it is necessary for your belief in any external teacher to disappear for only then can the comforter within you be found.

There is only one cause, only one I AM.

I, the trinity, in unthinkable origin, AM God the Father, and in creative expression AM the son, for imagination is born of consciousness. I, in universal

interpretation, in infinite imminence, in eternal procession AM God, the Holy Spirit. The real definition of
imminence is "sooner than now and nearer than here."
I AM, therefore, the comforter. What could comfort
you more than the knowledge that you don't have to
wait for your dreams to come true? They are nearer
than here and sooner than now. Let this knowledge be
your comforter.

*If there was a limit to that which is contained in
an infinite state, it would not be infinite.*

*As your belief in yourself grows,
your heart will find peace.*

*Turn your attention from want and lack
(all negative states) and place it on fulfillment
and abundance (positive states).*

*Your destination is always reached
by an internal direction.*

CHAPTER 12

The Human Spirit

The Bible tells of the human spirit's never-ending struggle to assert its supremacy over the natural mind. Believing in the reality of the world outside, the natural mind rules sleeping man, while the human spirit is God in man, struggling to awaken and assert its supremacy over all. The poet Faust knew this when he said, "Two souls are housed within my breast. One to Heaven doth aspire and the other to earth doth cling."

In the twenty-fifth chapter of Genesis this struggle is told as the story of Isaac's two sons, Esau and Jacob. Coming first as outer skin and hair, Esau is recognized as your personality, while the smooth-skinned Jacob is your human spirit. We are told that when their mother Rebekah became aware of the struggle within her, she questioned the Lord, who told her, "Two nations are in your womb and two people born of you shall be divided. One shall be stronger than the other, and the elder shall serve the younger."

Your external world is known by reason of your critical faculties; therefore, you can always discover the psychological state in which you reside by observing your thoughts of the day. Now, every state has its limitations and restrictions from which there appears to be no escape. If you believe you are the state in which you now reside, you will never be able to leave it. But the story of Esau and Jacob tells you there is a way of escape and how to accomplish it.

Esau exists in your mind as the outer world of fact, and Jacob as the inner world of imagination. As their father, you have the power to give either son the right of birth. Always seeing from where you have placed your attention, you are called upon to blind yourself to the outside world by drawing your attention from it, then deceiving yourself by imagining the world as you want it to be. This is done by closing your eyes to the so-called "facts" of life and turning your thoughts inward. Now, clothe your thoughts in the feeling of reality until they are just as solid and factual as those known to you by reason of your outer senses. When this is done, you, Isaac, have given your son Jacob the right of birth.

Your objective world is always reflecting your inner, subjective state. Therefore, it is impossible to change your outer world until you have changed your inner, subjective state. Knowing the state you want to occupy, completely absorb yourself in it as though it were a sponge and you the water capable of entering and being absorbed by it. Lose yourself in the feeling of satisfaction and fulfillment so, that when you open your eyes and Esau (the world without) returns, you know you have given his birthright away. Although you have been self-deceived by imagining the state to be real, you have given it the power to be born. How it is going to come about I do not know. Only your Father in Heaven knows, for he has ways to make your desired state alive and His ways are past finding out.

Now, there is an essence in you that is sound asleep and must be awakened. When you give Jacob the power you have given Esau, watch. You will discover that Esau will no longer react violently but will become passive. Then you will know that you have brought about a reversal of order. As you are aware of being

Jacob, you will persist in seeing what you want to see and experiencing what you want to express, thereby awakening your true essence to the truth that the world and all within it is yours.

You are the Rebekah the Bible tells about and you are constantly bringing forth your Esau and your Jacob, who are forever at war with each other. The elder is the world you know by reason of your critical faculties, while the younger is the one you know subjectively. The person you want to be is struggling for birth. As long as you look at and accept the outer world as the only reality, you will never give birth to your fulfilled desire. You must turn your attention inward and subjectively appropriate your objective reality.

When you read the twenty-fifth and twenty-seventh chapters of Genesis, remember, all the characters recorded there are in your mind. Although unmarried, you are always giving birth to twins. The world in which you live is the outpicturing of your state of awareness. That state is your first son, which must be supplanted by your second son, or desired state. Throughout the Bible, you will find there is always a second son who replaces the first: Jacob supplants Esau; Jesus supplants John the Baptist; and the human spirit supplants human matter.

When you know what you want, define it as vividly as you can. Then blind yourself to your externalized state by sending it hunting. You cannot touch your second son (your cherished idea) until you do. This is accomplished by turning your attention away from all thoughts of denial, and clothing your desire with the skins of reality. In his "Ode to a Nightingale," Keats wrote:

> "My heart aches, and a drowsy numbness
> pains my sense as
> Though of hemlock I have drunk."

Having felt the reality of his experience so vividly, when he opened his eyes, Keats asked:

> "Was it a vision, or a waking dream?
> Fled is that music: do I wake or sleep?"

It is with this kind of intensity that I would ask you to clothe yourself as you feel yourself already the person you want to be. Now, stretch out your imaginary hands and touch the objects there. Listen with your imaginary ears. See with your imaginary eyes. Walk in your imaginary world as you taste and smell the objects there. Your creative power can be used for anything, be it a fur coat or a new hat. It is my hope that you will use it for some noble state such as greatness in your chosen profession, whatever that may be. Now, let us look at the thirty-eighth chapter of Genesis and the story of Judah and Tamar. Judah means "praise" and Tamar means "a desired state, a palm tree oasis." As Tamar, you thirst for your desire. Give it to yourself by going into your desired state and making it real by becoming one with it. Feel the sense of satisfaction that your prayer has been answered and you are the woman called Tamar and the man named Judah.

You will find another account of twins in the forty-eighth chapter of Genesis. This is the story of Manasseh (which means "to forgive") and his brother Ephraim (which means "to affirm"). One is negation and the other affirmation. When you take your attention away from your problem by affirming its solution, the problem is momentarily forgotten. Persist in your affirmation, not in repetitious form, but in feeling. As you feel the solution, the problem dies from lack of attention.

This teaching is not for the complacent but for the human spirit who hungers and thirsts after right thinking. As we are told in the fifth chapter of Matthew, "Blessed are those who hunger and thirst after righteousness, for they shall be satisfied." Awaken the Jacob in you by observing your thoughts uncritically. Think of yourself as two beings, one who sees with the organs of sense and the other who sees through the mind of imagination. The man of sense is a creature of habit. He is dynamic and active; yet, through the daily practice of self-observation, he can be brought into a passive state and his power transferred to the man of imagination. There are always two decided outlooks on the same world, i.e., the one you see with your outer organs and the one you know only mentally. Your desire is mental, without shape or form. It is your second son, who will supplant your present world when your power of awareness is turned within.

Do you have a longing? A consuming desire that you want fulfilled now? Allow that desire to clothe your mind. Knowing that its fulfillment is based upon feeling, ask yourself what the feeling would be like if your desire were now realized. Whatever your problem is, its solution is within you. Turn your attention to your desire's fulfillment and clothe it in the skins of objective reality. This is the technique of reversal and should never be taken lightly, because the moment you feel yourself into a state, you instantly take upon yourself the fruit of that state.

I hope you now know how to clothe your subjective longing. Think of your desire as Jacob; then clothe it in the skins and hair of Esau. The time it takes for your longing to materialize is proportionate to your feeling of its naturalness.

The kingdom of Heaven is within you. Humanity cannot enter this kingdom, but your imagination can when you detach yourself from that to which you are now attached. There must be a separation, for only the human spirit is called, and only the human spirit can pass, singly, through this "I."

Now, that which requires a state of consciousness to produce its effect cannot be affected without such a state. Once you have entered a state, don't be concerned about how it will be externalized, for everything comes into being through consciousness. You never create a state. All states were created before the world was. Rather, you enter a state and it simply displays itself. Enter the state of poverty by saying, "I am poor" and you will see its evidence displayed on your screen of space. You do not generate health, wealth and happiness. The states are already there, completely furnished and ready for your immediate occupancy.

My words are true, but truth by itself can do nothing. It must be applied. Unapplied truth is like a lamp without oil, but applied truth is a lamp whose oil never runs low. Remember, there are no accidents, no cause other than an imaginal one. If an accident is fatal, it is an involuntary suicide. Are we not told, "No one takes my life, I lay it down myself. I have the power to lay it down and the power to take it up again." An accident is not a force external to the individual's consciousness. "No one knows a man but the spirit of the man who dwells in him," and man is simply the sum total of his reactions to life. No one comes into your world save you call him.

*You have the power to call anything into being,
for you are the author of the drama called life.*

*Knowing your desire, persist in the thought that you
already have it, until your thoughts become habitual.
If you do not, you will find yourself returning to
your old way of thinking and perpetuate it,
thereby never seeing your desire externalize itself.*

*Your objective world is always reflecting your inner,
subjective state.*

*Health, wealth and happiness are already there,
completely furnished and ready
for your immediate occupancy.*

CHAPTER 13

The Feeling of "I"

Your journey into this world of decay and death began with your feeling of "I" for wherever you place that feeling, there you live. You can place your feeling of "I" in the mud of negation or on the lovely ground of positive assumption. Your feeling of "I" is always with you. It is your slave and your savior, for wherever you go, there "I" am also.

The ninth chapter of Numbers begins with Moses being given instructions by the Lord about how to erect a tabernacle, or tent of testimony, and move it across the desert. He was told: "During the day a cloud will cover the tabernacle, and at night it will have the appearance of a pillar of fire. Whenever the cloud rises, the children of Israel must journey to the place where the cloud settles down, there the people must remain. It may rise once a week, once a month or longer, but when it ascends, the children of Israel must journey."

Now, a tabernacle is an elongated place of worship that is movable and covered with skin. You are that temple (tabernacle), and the spirit of God dwells within you as your "I." A cloud is a garment of water (or psychological truth) that covers the "I" and that to which it testifies. The cloud does not move in time but is lifted up by the "I" it covers. According to my senses, "I" am now in the Palace Hotel. Let me lift the cloud from my testament by withdrawing the feeling of "I" from the evidence of my senses and move by placing my "I" in a predetermined state, and my whole world moves with me. Clothing myself in feeling, the cloud covers me as I testify to the state I have just entered. At this moment, you may have placed your feeling of "I" in an unlovely state and, unless you lift that cloud that covers you, you are anchored there and are incapable of changing the circumstances of your life. Now, this lifting of the cloud and placing your feeling of "I" in a more desirable state involves a death, for when the cloud rises, it breaks (or kills) the cycle of recurrence you have been on.

Motion can be detected only as a change of position with respect to another body, and all motion spoken of in scripture is psychological. Every state exists in this psychological land from which your "I" journeys. All you need do is extract your "I" from where it is now and place it in your predetermined state. But how will you know you have moved? By using a frame of reference. While sitting quietly in your chair, you can lift your cloud by placing the feeling of "IF" in an entirely different psychological state. No one can see this motion, for yours is a spiritual journey. While in the state, look for confirmation of your move on the faces of people there. Are they surprised to see you? Are they happy for you? A little jealous? Look, until you see the expressions on their faces. If there is a change in your feeling of "I," you will find an automatic alteration in your usual expression of life.

During the day, you wear your garment of truth (the cloud); but the moment you begin to meditate, the brain grows luminous. This is the pillar of fire by night. Remember, "I AM the truth," and wherever you place your feeling of "I," there you must abide.

In the thirty-fourth chapter of Deuteronomy we are told that Moses went up from the plains of Moab to

Nebo, and there to Pisgah, which is opposite Jericho, where he was shown all the land that was his. The word Moses means "to draw out." He is not a man but your creative power that can draw out of you any state you have placed your "I," struck the rock and produced the water.

The word Moab means "mother/father," which is your "I AMness." In your present state, your Moab may be saying, "I am beaten," "I am sick," "I am impoverished." But Nebo means "to prophesy your longing by the feeling of I." Pisgah means "to contemplate." When you enter your desired state, observe your Jericho, for it will have a fragrant odor, as that is what the word Jericho means. Having risen in consciousness, remain in your chosen state until you have a reaction that satisfies you. A violent reaction produces a horrible odor, while a lovely reaction indicates Jericho and a lovely odor. You see, Jericho is not a place in the Near East, but a state that produces the thrill of accomplishment within you.

In the fourteenth chapter of the Book of John, Jesus speaks to Peter, saying, "Let not your heart be troubled; you believe in God, believe also in me. In my Father's house are many rooms; if it were not so would I have told you that I go to prepare a place for you? And when I go and prepare a place for you I will come again and take you to myself, that where I am, you may be also."

This is not a man speaking to another, but self-speaking to self. You are Jesus (imagination) telling yourself that there are unnumbered states of awareness for you to enter, and you are inviting self to choose the state you wish to inhabit. After selecting the state, imagination will go and prepare it for you so that you may come again (as you must), for wherever you abide in imagination, there you shall reside also in the flesh. If you believe what I have told you, determine to change your feeling of "I." There is no power that can keep you from realizing your dream, but you! And no man can compel you to enter any state. You have the power to select your state and enter it, thereby making it alive, or leave a state, thereby killing it. The decision (and its consequences) is yours and yours alone. The day you can become an observing "I," watching your reactions and seeing the observer and the thing observed as two distinct beings, you will know you can enter any state and it will outpicture itself. You will know that all the mansions of your Father's house are yours.

I AM (consciousness) contains the whole of creation, and out of I AMness comes imagination. Where there is no consciousness, there is no imagination. When you enter a state, your I AM is having a psychological experience. When you think about a state, you have a subject and its object; but when you experience a state, you have unification.

*The teaching of truth deals with the feeling of "I,"
for only through feeling can change come about.*

*If you continue to have the same reactions,
you have not changed your feelings.*

*Your world forever conforms
to your inner assumption.*

Out of I AMness comes imagination.

CHAPTER 14

The Wine of Eternity

The human imagination and Divine Imagination are one and the same. They are not two. Your human imagination has the power to turn your water of life into the wine of eternity. This you will do when you release your imagination from its bonds of limitation, for when imagination is truly free, it can accomplish miracles.

The Bible calls imagination man's savior and identifies this wonderful benefactor as Christ. When Christ is awakened and born in you, your human imagination becomes divine vision. Called Christ, your individual imagination is the mediator between the Father of all life and the external world called Man. Having imagined wealth, it is the human imagination who walks on the water of life and denies the evidence of his senses by claiming, "I am wealthy." His persistence mediates God to Man.

Every character in scripture lives in the mind. When you read the Bible, turn to self and ask, "What state would I be in if I were doing this?" When reading the story of Moses, claim you are he. Assume the state of faith when you read of Abraham. You are Joseph, the dreamer, and Thomas, the doubter; and you are destined to be Jesus Christ, the awakened, Risen Imagination.

Skin is the most external thing a man can wear. When you read of one who wears camel's hair or leather, you are reading of one whose mind is tied to the outside. His philosophy of life is external and dependent entirely on others. In the fifth chapter of Mark, the story is told of an innocent man who, being unclothed, lived among the dead and cut himself on the stones. When Awakened Imagination passed by, the innocent one cried out, "Do not cast me out." And when asked his name, he answered, "My name is Legion, for we are many."

A being not yet individualized in a spiritual sense is innocent, for he knows not what he is doing. He is

Legion because he has innumerable "Is" in him, i.e., "I am ill," "I am poor," "I am tired," "I am weak" and "I am mistreated," to name but a few. Living among the dead and sleeping the sleep of death, his literal understanding of life and its cause are stones that cut and bruise. But the spiritual man has a personal self-determined history, a predetermined self. In the realm of the spirit, he becomes what he wills. When consciousness turns within, the spirit awakens to his true identity. Then, casting out all belief in any external cause, he is clothed in his right mind and sits at the foot of the one who cast them out.

A miracle is only the name given by those who have no faith in the works of faith. The story is told of a man named Jairus whose daughter was believed to be dead. But Awakened Imagination ignored the thought and said, "Do not fear, only believe." Arriving at the house, he questioned, "Why do you weep? The child is not dead, but sleeping." Then he touched the child and said, "I say to you, rise." Immediately, she got up and walked. Then Jesus turned to the parents and said, "Give her something to eat."

Every state, every desire, every idea is your child. Looking at the desire, it appears to be dead to you, the natural man. But your spiritual "I" knows the desire is not dead, but sleeping, waiting to be touched for its resurrection. With your desire (child) made alive within you through the power of touch, it must be fed in order to bring about its birth. This is done by turning your attention to it.

Now let us turn to the fifth chapter of the Book of John, in which he speaks of the pool of Bethesda and its five porches. The story is told of a sick man who waits for the moving of the water by an angel, believing that whoever steps into the pool first, after the movement, will be healed. After asking him if he wanted to be healed, Awakened Imagination said, "Rise, take up your pallet and walk," and at once the man was healed, and taking up his pallet, he walked away.

The word Bethesda means "house of mercy." And the pool spoken of here is consciousness, which must be stirred by an angel (a messenger of God). Any idea you entertain is that angel, disturbing your consciousness. The pool is entered by a mere assumption, and stirred as you bathe in it. "I AM" is always first person, present tense. No one can put you in the pool by affirmation. Although seemingly impotent, you rest on the five porches, or senses, when you accept their evidence and refuse to change your consciousness. No one need help you. Who could be first in the pool other than self, which is your "I"? Knowing what you want, rise in the assumption that your desire is already satisfied (healed) and it will be.

In his seventeenth chapter, John rejoices, saying, "I have finished the work thou gavest me to do. Father, glorify thou me in thine own self with the glory which I had with thee before that the world was. I have kept them in thy name which thou hast given me and none is lost but the son of perdition. For their sake, I consecrate myself that they also may be consecrated in the truth, for I dwell in them and they dwell in me and we are one."

The work you gave yourself to do is to awaken from this dream of life. Having assumed the limitations of the flesh, you will awaken to your true identity and become your own glory when the outer you is made passive and the inner you, dynamic. Now, the son of perdition is the belief in loss. Knowing that all things exist in the human imagination, nothing can be lost. When you realize this truth, you will no longer believe in loss, thereby fulfilling scripture.

The most difficult thing to grasp is that there is no one outside of self. Believing others needed to change, I worked on them, thinking that the world would be so much better if they would be different. Then I awoke

and sanctified myself, and in so doing, they were sanctified, for I dwell in them and they dwell in me and
we are one. There is no one to change but self. As you
control your thoughts and allow only those that conform to your ideal to flow from you, your world will
reshape itself in harmony with them. Remember, you
cannot be aware of a fault or greatness in another were
that fault or greatness not present in you. Remove the
fault from your own "I." Place the greatness there and
watch your world change as it reflects your change in
consciousness.

In the sixteenth chapter of Matthew, the disciples
were questioned, "Who do men say the son of man is?"
They said, "Some say John the Baptist, others Elijah
and others Jeremiah, or one of the prophets." Then he
asked, "But who do you say that I AM?" Simon Peter
replied, "You are the Christ, the Son of the living God."

At the present time, you may be concerned about
what others think of you, but when you have awakened
to your true divinity, it will not matter to you what others think. You will know from experience that you are
the Christ, the Son of the living God. Flesh and blood
will not reveal this to you, but your Father who is in
Heaven reveals it. Through this knowledge, you will
have been given the keys to the kingdom, and what-

ever you bind on Earth will be bound in Heaven, and whatever you loose on Earth will be loosed in Heaven. Having found the answer to the everlasting question, "Who am I?" no man can ever take this knowledge from you. This wisdom comes from within.

Completely abandon yourself to a psychological experience. If you become one with a state in your imagination, you will rise to encompass it in the flesh. This being true, yours is a journey from innocence to imagination to experience.

You are already the person you want to be. Claim it and tomorrow you will display it by being it. By your fruits you shall be known.

If today your life is not what you want it to be, stop blaming anyone; just keep working on changing your feeling of "I" and abide in your desired state. Persist . . . persist . . . persist, for at the moment of non-reaction, circumstances change. We rise by an energy others call effort, for it takes energy to act and react. All through the day, remember your aim by constantly identifying yourself with it. Let your reactions flow into your aim. Ask for deeper and deeper understanding of that which you think you now understand. I trust everyone has an aim to be greater. Do not limit yourself to any textbook. Stop believing that any one man can write a book that is final regarding truth. Start to dig. No one can grow without outgrowing. A different attitude is the solution to every problem. By your new direction (attitude) you escape that which has been wrapped around you. There is no one to change but self, so start changing yourself today!

Luke was speaking of you when he made this statement: "When their eyes were opened, they recognized him and he vanished from their sight."

When your "I" is awakened, you will find that which you have been searching for, and the belief in a power outside of self will disappear. In Francis Thompson's poem, "The Hound of Heaven," he tells of how:

> "I fled Him, down the nights and down the days;
> I fled Him, down the arches of the years;
> I fled Him, down the labyrinthine ways
> Of my own mind ..."

only to discover at the end that "He was my very self."

Man's eyes are blind, though hounded constantly by the Hound of Heaven. He cannot believe in the non-historicity of the Bible but continues to hold onto his little beliefs even though he does not know what to do with them. People do not seek truth; they seek only supports for their opinions of it. But I say to you, "Do not think that I have come to bring peace on Earth; I have not come to bring peace, but a sword. I have come to set a man against his father and a daughter against her mother and a daughter-in-law against her mother-in-law, for a man's foes are those of his own household." When truth comes, it sets a man at war with himself, for he will discover that he can no longer consent to what he formerly believed in.

*Start now and quietly listen to the words
you want to hear.*

No one can grow without outgrowing.

*By a new direction, internally, you can change
the course of your life and free yourself
from the prisons of your mind.*

*The human imagination and Divine Imagination
are one and the same.*

CHAPTER 15

Awake, O Sleeper

I n the Book of Ephesians we are told to "Awake, O sleeper, and arise from the dead, and Christ shall give you light." This awakening and rising comes about through an inner development, for the Bible is your autobiography. It was you who inspired the prophets to record their visions. And it is you who will fulfill their prophecies in a first-person, present-tense experience. As you read the Bible, get your mental teeth into it. Study its message, and your understanding will go deeper and deeper as you travel through life.

The Bible teaches self-help. Do not look to any leader on the outside, only look to self by turning within. If anyone offers to do for you what you can do for yourself, reject their offer and turn to Christ, God's creative power in you, who is your life, your light of the world. By changing your thinking, Christ will change your world.

The "earth," spoken of in scripture, is the "mind of man." It is in this psychological earth that the idea of the kingdom of Heaven was implanted. While in the state of sleep, false doctrines have crept in. Called tares, they grow with the wheat and will be harvested; therefore, you must become selective and clear the weeds by killing every belief in a power outside the mind.

The man who is rich is complacent. Satisfied with his social and financial positions, he is not hungry to grow. If you are complacent, your life will not change, for you will not be hungry or thirst for a higher level of awareness. You and you alone know whether the hunger has come upon you or not; but you have not begun the work you gave yourself to do until you begin to uncritically observe your thoughts. And when you do, you will discover that you are not as truthful, honest or courageous as you thought you were.

Tonight, select a future upon which you want to work, and tomorrow, be watchful. Question yourself by saying, "Am I keeping the tense? Do I want this? Is that the way my friend wants me to see him? Am I limiting myself?" Then act in your imagination, for imagination is passive while asleep and allows that which is false to take the throne. Watch your thoughts. Reclaim your throne and consciously allow your human imagination to rule your world!

Your human imagination, once activated, will awaken as a little babe. Born in violence, in a manger where the wild beasts eat, it will grow in wisdom and power as the outer you will become passive and powerless. But you must be watchful and vigilant of your thoughts in order to bring the outer you into passivity. Only then will you know what it is like to be in the world but not of it. The purpose of this teaching is to awaken the Christ who is asleep in man, dreaming different states into being, and bring him to the conscious circle of humanity where man is self-aware. Once you are aware of your true self, you will no longer condemn sleeping man. You will know they are machines, automatons who do not know what they are doing.

Your desires are not subjective, intangible things, but solidly real. Begin to awaken the Christ in you by clothing your subjective desires in objective reality. I promise you, the day you do this, they will become facts in your world. Have an aim that you will not lie to yourself anymore. Work on this feature within yourself. Become extremely observant and honest with yourself and watch the energy that formerly moved into negative states, flow into your greater aim. Perhaps your aim is to become a great teacher, not because you want to impose your will upon others, but because you want to awaken in others what you have awakened in yourself. The awakening begins when you feel a separation; a division of the natural and the spiritual imaginative you to which all things are possible. It is this spiritual you that clothes your subjective state in reality.

By changing the feeling of "I," you can direct your life internally and escape the prison of your present state regardless of what it may be. By thinking from the point of view that the problem is solved, you move from the problem to its solution. This change of attitude is called the "be-attitudes." In other words, you are "being" what you want to be by assuming that you already are it. When you know what you want, consciously clothe yourself in a new concept of self by extracting your "I" from the evidence of the senses and placing it in the place you want to be. By this assumption (or be-attitude), you have journeyed from one state to another. "And I, if I be lifted up, I draw all men to me."

Once you have lifted yourself up into the new

states, abide there! Do not come back to the testimonies of your senses, but remain in your desire until a different world is established. Every change in the feeling of "I" automatically produces changes in the external world; therefore, you must learn to die daily in regards to your old beliefs. The statement, "Those who lose their life for my sake will find it," means letting go of all that you now consent to. If you lose it, you will find your "I" reclothing itself on a higher level of being, thereby causing a new expression in your world.

When you go in a new direction, the journey is made in the mind. A physical journey may follow, but the journey must be made on the inside first. Where you are, is what you psychologically are at that moment. An enlightened being lives on the mountaintop and the human imagination, when completely controlled, is personified as a being called Jesus Christ.

As long as you are violent, you are asleep. Awaken the spiritual you by watching your actions and reactions to life, and you will lose your impulse to retaliate. What happens to you here is not important, but how you react to what happens, is. Your reactions define you. They tell you where you are, for you attract life in its most minute detail.

The Bible does not teach reincarnation. Its central

teaching is the rebirth of consciousness into ever higher and higher levels. You must be born by water and spirit, not water only. Except for the man born of spirit, he cannot enter the higher level of being called the kingdom of Heaven. In this series of lectures, you have received psychological instruction about how to go about working on yourself. Your mind has been washed of certain errors, baptized and born of water. But, unless this truth is applied, you will not be born of the spirit.

The word Mary means "water." Christ, the "I" in you, is born of water and of the Holy Spirit. The outer you cannot receive instructions. He is literal and takes things literally, thereby receiving nothing but stone. The righteous man, however, is conscious of being the man he wants to be, while the foolish man steals from himself by not claiming his desire. Every time you see a man less than what he wants to be, you have robbed him of the state necessary to externalize it.

Be not as the heathen who by vain repetition hopes he can get the ear of God. Rather, when you pray, go within and close the door, and your Father who hears in secret will reward you openly. You have but to change the feeling of "I." Close the door to the outer world and feel yourself into the state your friend desires. With a planned program, see him and talk to him from the premise that he is that person already. Keep the door of reason and logic closed and walk in faith that what you have heard and seen, in secret, will be rewarded openly, and it will.

The Bible was written by the conscious circle of humanity. (You enter this circle at the moment of wakefulness.) Not composed by men, the Bible is divine instruction with limitless interpretations. It is a test in the development of your understanding and, as you grow, its understanding deepens and deepens.

Although man wraps himself in conditions (states), his true being is I AM. Anything man will consent to, he will manifest in his world. Can you accept as fact what your reason and senses deny? Or must you always bow to reason's dictates? The same consciousness that produces health, produces sickness, wealth and poverty. Whatever you agree to be conscious of, whatever you affirm as true, you will manifest.

All knees must bow to imagination. "Behold! We are transformed into the same image." Can you behold a given situation and make it so natural that you are transformed into its image? You can when you, all imagination, feel the naturalness of the image you behold.

Divinity is not divided; therefore, everyone is but a projection of the one. You are told to love your neighbors as yourself, for there is no other. Sanctify self, not another. Working on others will not change them; only by changing yourself will others change. Seek confirmation of your ideas and you are not growing. All textbooks are manmade and uninspired from on high. Stick to them and you will remain on their level. Believe in self! Trust your human imagination and you will grow in wisdom and in stature, and, as you grow, you will outgrow your former beliefs.

We are God's children, destined to be God himself,
and God creates everything He,
individualized as you, consents to.

Resolve only to hear what is good concerning yourself
and another, so everything that enters your mind will
contribute to a life of joy, feasting on higher states.

Divinity is not divided; therefore,
everyone is but a projection of the One.

When you know the spiritual being within you,
you will assert the supremacy of imagination.

DeVorss Publications has proudly published the wisdom of Neville Goddard for more than 80 years!

The Word of Neville
A Compilation of Wisdom and Imagination

NEVILLE GODDARD
Collected and Edited by Natalia Larson

Here is a unique collection of life-changing quotes from Neville Goddard that contains many never-before published spoken selections. THE WORD OF NEVILLE offers prolific and transformative excerpts from his numerous books, lectures, and talks which include original bits of wisdom that were never printed in his books. Gathered from recordings, Natalia Larson has extracted the brilliance of Neville, and now DeVorss is releasing this very unique book for Neville fans to hold close and cherish. For over 80 years, DeVorss Publications has proudly published the remarkable wisdom of Neville Goddard. This long and prosperous relationship began with YOUR FAITH IS YOUR FORTUNE in 1941 in a small office near 9th and Grand in downtown Los Angeles, and continues to this day with books like THE POWER OF YOUR UNLIMITED IMAGINATION.

"Neville captured the sheer logic of creative mind principles. His work impacted me in a very profound way; in fact, he's been a great mentor to me." ~ DR. WAYNE DYER

Neville's wisdom and spiritual guidance continues to resonate in the world today. For those seeking the strength and courage to change from within, here's a book they can keep at their side every step of the way.

Pocket Paperback 220pg
ISBN: 9780875169200

Other Books by Neville

AWAKENED IMAGINATION
9780875166568
Includes *The Search*

THE POWER OF AWARENESS
9780875166551

YOUR FAITH IS YOUR FORTUNE
9780875160788

IMMORTAL MAN
9780875167237

THE LAW AND THE PROMISE
9780875165325

RESURRECTION
9780875168258

THE NEVILLE READER
9780875168111
Includes
The Law and the Promise
Prayer, the Art of Believing
Feeling Is the Secret
Resurrection
Freedom for All
Out of This World
Seedtime and Harvest

For more information, please visit www.devorss.com
or call 800-843-5743

Printed in the USA
CPSIA information can be obtained
at www.ICGtesting.com
JSHW082353140824
68134JS00020B/2065